THE
VALLEY OF OAXACA

SALVAT

TEXT
Juan Carlos Muñoz

ACADEMIC SUPERVISION
Lina Odena Güemes

EDITORIAL COORDINATION
Ma. Guadalupe Casillas

DESIGN AND ILLUSTRATIONS
Sergio Arzate
Hilda Sánchez

FHOTOGRAPHS
Ignacio Urquiza
Archivo Salvat

PHOTOGRAPHIE
David Castledine

First printed 1992

PRINTED IN 1992 BY:
Gráficas Monte Albán, S.A. de C.V.
Municipio El Marqués, Querétaro

Impreso en México
Printed in México

Promotora Editorial, S.A. de C.V.
Presidente Masaryk 101-5o. piso
México, D.F.
ISBN 970-611-253-7

This first edition consists
of 3,000 copies with additional
replacement.

Contents

General Information

To reach the archaeological sites in the Valley of Oaxaca, take the road that leaves the Barrio San Juanico in San Martín de Mexicapan, seven kilometers from the state capital. Admission is very reasonable (discount for students). Open Tuesday through Sunday, 9 a.m. to 5 p.m. For further information, phone 5-04-00, 5-00-02 or 5-63-89.

Historical stages

The Valley of Oaxaca, together with Puebla and part of Veracruz made up the central region of Mesoamerica. This fact alone gave it, and especially Monte Albán, strategic importance. Its position —at cultural crossroads— made it easy for this valley to receive influences from several regions bordering on it such as Teotihuacán, the Maya area and the Olmec zone.

The Valley of Oaxaca (in fact composed of three interconnecting valleys) lies in the middle of the State. Surrounded by the Sierra de Juárez, it has fertile land and a temperate climate. Several ethnic and linguistic groups live there, of which two are particularly important: the Zapotecs and the Mixtecs.

Historical study of it is divided into five periods, and very often, because Monte Albán is the most representative site in this area, these periods are given the name of this city: Monte Albán I, II, III, etc. However, some experts such as Ignacio Bernal suggest the periods should be named Oaxaca I, II, III, etc. This second possibility is actually both fairer and more

Great square of Monte Albán, hub of the Oaxaca Valley.

accurate because historical processes occur over all the region, not only in Monte Albán.

There is evidence that man was already living in the valley in 8,000 B.C., although it is impossible to know who they were and what language they spoke. Towards 2,000 B.C., agriculture began and, parallel to this, a sedentary existence. Small settlements make their appearance, pottery is born, obsidian, hard minerals, shells brought from the sea are worked, mirrors are made of magnetite.

The historical importance of the valley begins however in the seventh century B.C. From then until the arrival of the Spanish in 1519 we have a period of more than two thousand years of uninterrupted evolution. We shall examine this history more fully later.

Interest in studying the Valley of Oaxaca began in Colonial times. Francisco de Burgoa mentions Mitla in his *Geográfica Descriptiva*, which must have then been in a good state of preservation. Monte Albán was covered by vegetation.

In 1806 William Dupaix, a French-born Hungarian and Luciano Castañeda gave the first known description of Monte Albán. Later, between 1831 and 1848 Dupaix

would continue to report on finds at Mitla and Zaachila. In 1853 Juan Bautista Carriedo produced a plan of Monte Albán and a drawing of the five "dancers" discovered by Dupaix. José Murguía y Galindo, governor of the State of Oaxaca, published a brief description of Monte Albán in 1861. Then, in the last two decades of the last century, the area was visited successively by Johann von Müller, Desiré Charnay, Adolphe F. Bandelier and William H. Holmes. This last visitor produced magnificent descriptions of the architecture and ceramics of Monte Albán. Interest had by now been aroused in exploring the area, especially Monte Albán. So it was that Dr. Sologuren and the lawyer Belmar excavated Mound L, discovering eight more figures where Dupaix had found the first five "dancers". In the twentieth century Leopoldo Batres went to Monte Albán in 1901 and considered it a "sacerd city"; he cleared the site generally and recovered five more carvings of "dancers". However, the first archaeologist to mount a real project to study Monte Albán was Alfonso Caso, who in 1931 began a series of 18 seasons of archaeological digs. Thanks to him and to the later

In the post-Classic, the Mixtecs brought the city of Mitla to its height.

investigations of Ignacio Bernal and Jorge R. Acosta we now have a fairly clear idea of developments in the Valley of Oaxaca.

As mentioned earlier, five very distinct periods are to be seen in the history of the Valley. We shall take a brief look at them.

Valley of Oaxaca I. This covers the period 800 to 150 B.C. Trade in raw materials (articles in shell, jade and pyrites) had begun to bring movement to the region. Revealed religion with permanent temples exists by this time, an organized cult and a well-defined priestly hierarchy. There is also evidence of the first tombs built of stone (presumably for high-ranking persons). Architecture and urban planning have a characteristic design based on three features: stone bases and platforms around courtyards and squares; the use of vertical walls and superimposed stairways on each of the faces; columns to support roofs. Stucco is also used as a covering for walls. However, almost nothing survives of the architecture of this epoch. Also belonging to the Valley of Oaxaca I phase are the

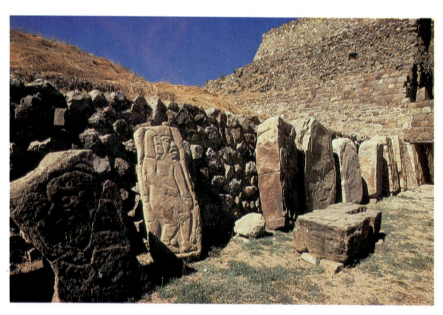

Carvings known as "Dancers". Valley of Oaxaca I.

8

carvings known as "dancers": large stones decorated with human figures in a wide variety of positions and attitudes that give them this name. Incidentally, the "dancers" are all male figures that have given rise to several different interpretations. The figures are naked, with open mouths and wide, squat noses; their eyes are sometimes open and sometimes not (perhaps denoting life and death) and their legs and arms are strangely elongated. They possibly represent not dancers but prisoners, especially because nakedness was a humiliating form of punishment. We shall later see other interpretations of their meaning.

Finally, the first forms of the calendar and writing make their appearance in this period. A bas-relief with glyphs dating from 7 B.C. discovered in San José Mogote leads to this supposition. This site, and Monte Albán are best documented for the study of this stage. At this time, Monte Albán had between 10,000 and 20,000 inhabitants.

Valley of Oaxaca II. This runs from 150 B.C. to 300 B.C. In this period, though there were no great changes, we can see elements that were not present in the preceding period. In architecture for example the changes were minimal —only the use of the lintel. Vertical walls (tablero) were still built but the sloping base wall (talud) and ramps

Bas relief with calendar glyphs from San José Mogote.

had yet to make their appearance (to come in the following stage). But arrivals from Chiapas introduced a novelty: arrow-shaped buildings, such as the one at Caballito Blanco, near Yagul. In the field of sculpture, stelae were erected (perhaps derived

9

Jade mask of the Bat god. Valley of Oaxaca II.

xicalcoliuhqui, which is a stepped fret pattern symbolizing a serpent, begins to feature. There is also evidence of a well-established Bat God, of whom jade figures have been found.

Edifice J is the most representative of this period. The population remained more or less the same.

Valley of Oaxaca III. This period covers 300 A.D. to 700-750 A.D. The most notable feature of it is the presence of influence from Teotihuacán. During these years, Teotihuacán imposes many cultural forms that are adopted throughout almost the whole of Mesoamerica, including the Oaxaca valleys area. This cultural sign, imported from the great city on the High Plateau, is particularly noticeable in architecture. The most remarkable feature is the generalized use of the "talud-tablero" (plain sloping walls alternating with vertical surfaces decorated with a cornice or a frame) that give the city a special look. Also originating from Teotihuacán is the staircase as an integral part of the building (i.e. not superimposed). Another point to note is that at the time, many of the pyramid-like monuments were painted red.

Together with the buildings, many stelae were erected which bear long, hieroglyphic inscriptions in bas-relief that have not been deciphered so far. Zapotec culture was at its height in these years; Monte Albán

from the Olmecs) and in pottery the characteristic design of platters with four hollow, bulbous supports appears, and urns portraying deities. Also, in symbiotic relationship with pottery, a decorative motif known as

Mitla, another important center of the Zapotec-Mixtec culture.

contained some 35,000 inhabitants, the half of Teotihuacán's population, and there were 38 distinct deities, including 11 goddesses. The Ball Court at Monte Albán probably belongs to this period.

Valley of Oaxaca IV. 800 - 1521 A.D. At some time between 750 and 800 A.D. Monte Albán began to decline until it definitely ceased to be the capital of the region. Its fall is linked firstly to the decline of Teotihuacán (beginning around 650 A.D.) and secondly to an increase in population. We are facing the decline of Zapotec culture. Some experts such as Paddock and Bernal maintain that the city was not destroyed, as apparently happened

to Tula, but abandoned, being turned into a necropolis only used as a sacred place for ceremonies.

The fall of Monte Albán, in contrast to that of Teotihuacán, was not caused by fire or any other catastrophe; it was a slow process of abandonment that ended in 800 A.D., by when there was no organized population.

In counterpart, other neighboring "chiefdoms" such as Zaachila, Cuilapan, Yagul and Mitla began to acquire importance, but of course there is no indications of a heyday.

Shapes in architecture and pottery remain more or less the same as in the preceding period, although there are already signs of artistic decadence. However, this stage is not sufficiently explored, mainly because there are almost no vestiges in Monte Albán. There are however good examples of sculpture at Lambityeco, where splendid stucco friezes depicting human and divine figures have been discovered.

Valley of Oaxaca V. The last stage begins in 1200 A.D. with the arrival of the Mixtecs and concludes in 1521 when the Spanish conquistadors came. Immediately notable is the fact that periods IV and V coincide, because Zapotecs and Mixtecs were living in the

Calendar glyphs can be seen on the headdress and chest of the "Youth of Cuilapan".

region at the same time. Valley of Oaxaca V refers particularly to the cultural modifications brought by the Mixtecs.

The changes are striking: an obvious preference for building mansions —called palaces because of their size and rich decoration— in preference to temples. There are also mosaics designed for both interior and exterior walls based on a wide range of stones carved and joined with masterly precision. For example, in one building at Mitla, more than 100,000 stones were used.

Two more elements are absolutely characteristic of Mixtec culture:

Mosaic designs on walls in an architectural feature of the Mixtec culture.

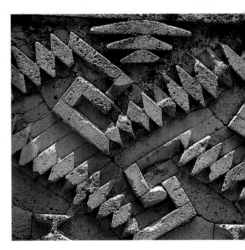

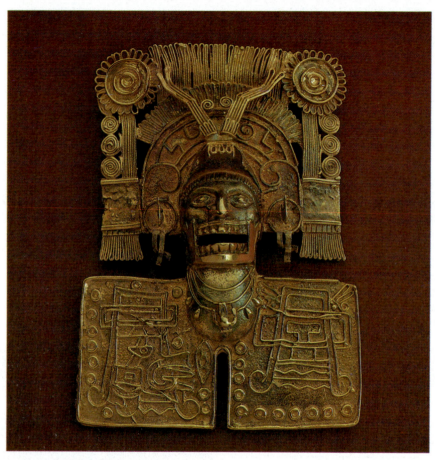

Gold was handled in masterly way by Mixtec craftsmen.

pottery and metalwork. The first is completely different from Zapotec, and the second makes its first appearance. There were obviously excellent jewlers, goldsmiths and potters.

By this time, Mitla and Zaachila were the capitals of the valley, although Tilantongo, Nochistlán, Tlacolula and Tlaxiaco had gained importance. But the region looked different without the splendor of past centuries. It was a dislocated zone.

Monte Albán

Without any doubt, the most highly developed site in the Valley of Oaxaca is Monte Albán, and so it is the most important zone for investigation. It is also one of the most monumental sites in Mesoamerica, and probably Monte Albán was the most ancient city in America, preceding all the other great cities of Mesoamerica.

It is located 14 km from the city of Oaxaca, 400 m above sea level. We do not know what its native name was, although it possibly meant "Hill of the Jaguar". We shall now examine the most important buildings in the city.

The Ball Court. This was most probably built in period III. It is shaped like the letter I and lies on a

Monte Albán is probably the oldest city in América.

15

A special feature of the Ball Court at Monte Albán is the use of sloping platforms.

north-south axis. Along the sides of the playing area are platforms with sloping sides (talud), and at each end, vertical walls. At each corner there is a small niche, whose use or function is not clear. Possibly, the image of the patron god was placed there, or perhaps the wagers. At this center of the court is a circular stone, possibly where the ball was thrown at the beginning of play. Strangely, the court has no stone hoops (the targets). Finally, at the top of the "talud" there is a zoomorphic figure that apparently represents a grasshopper.

Structure or Building P. This belongs to the Valley of Oaxaca III period and was found in a very poor state of preservation. However, some features can still be seen: it is built with the typical scapular panel (not Teotihuacán) and is separated from neighboring buildings by low platforms. It contains an astronomical reference to the so-called observatory in the Central

Group that we shall see later. Between Building P and the Central Group stands the only altar on the square. This building is not very striking, perhaps because of its ruined state.

The Palace or Structure S. The special feature of this building is that it was a dwelling. Inside there are 13 rooms around a central court, and perhaps this is why it is known as The Palace. On the front it has a staircase that is wider than the facade, ending at a small entrance that still has its lintel. A tomb was discovered under the courtyard and this fact, together with the building's residential look, leads to the supposition that it was where high-ranking persons lived.

South Platform. Here we are in the presence of monumental architecture, though a little less impressive than the North Platform

Building P is directly related to the observatory in the Central Group.

opposite. The platform is rectangular and faces north. The structure has not been thoroughly explored, which explains why not much is known about its interior architecture. Offerings and carved stones were found at three of its corners. Two of these stones were placed, intentionally it appears, with the carved portion face down. One of these is in the National Museum of Anthropology, and the other at the foot of this building. It would be very interesting to know the meaning of the glyphs on the stones, but the system of writing is still a mystery.

Structure M. This is a double construction: it has two rectangular bases with the main facade looking east. Its four sections are connected by wide staircases and ramps finishing in vertical walls with flat-molded panels. At the top are the remains of a temple. Between the two structures is a rectangular courtyard surrounded by high, narrow platforms. In the center of the courtyard stands a square-based altar.

Structure L or The Dancers. Although there seems to be only a single platform, there was actually a previous construction. Building of the present one began in Period I. The name, of course, comes from the stone slabs with human figures in relief. There are four rows of "dancers": in the first, the figures are upright with their faces turned to the right; in the third, also made of vertical slabs, they look left; in the horizontal rows between these two, the figures known as "swimmers" lie with faces turned to the right. Note that the figures are naked, their mouths half-open, their noses wide and squat; their eyes are sometimes open and sometimes closed, and their arms and legs are peculiarly long. What do these figures represent? Perhaps, because they are naked, which was a humiliating punishment, they are prisoners. There are also many remains of hieroglyphic writing and astronomical signs here. This reminds us of the Zapotec culture's advances in the calendar. However, some archaeologists reject this interpretation, arguing that in a sacred city like Monte Albán the figures are more likely to represent ritual activities than any to do with war. Piña Chan believes that the nudity of the figures is related to fertility cults, or even to a phallic cult of Olmec origin. In addition, the fact that they are found in association with hieroglyphic writing and astronomical signs seems to be connected to a story that recounts origins and describes primal personalities (ancestors, men-gods, heads of lines). Nevertheless, this suggestion is also based on certain amount of speculation.

The Central Group was probably an astronomical observatory.

Structure 4. This building has a striking resemblance to Structure M: it is a double construction with rectangular-based platforms and faces east; the sections are connected by wide staircases with ample ramps and, lastly, between the two bases lies a rectangular court surrounded by high, narrow platforms. In the northern part of the structure is Stele 18 (a little over 5 meters high), with calendar glyphs on both faces. This stone fell some

Remains of hieroglyphic writing and astronomical signs are connected with the "Dancers".

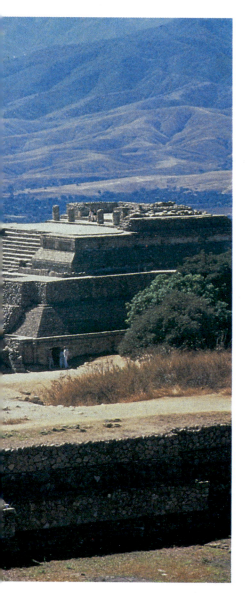

time in the past, and the pieces were rejoined, but the glyphs are now very obscured. Although several numbers can be made out (7, 5 and 9 monkey), any further reading is impossible. The Structure belongs to Period II.

North Platform. This is the result of a long building process. It faces south, and the facade has two vertical faces where carved monuments from earlier periods are incorporated. On the platform there are several smaller structures, among which the most interesting is the portico with double columns that leads into a large sunken courtyard with staircases on each of its four sides. In this 50,000-meter- square inner courtyard is an altar. Also, on the east side stands a construction known as Mound A and, on the west another, Mound B. This last, which belongs to Valley of Oaxaca V, is especially interesting because of its Mixtec architectural features.

Central Group. Of the buildings of the Central Group, Structure J stands alone in the south, and its orientation differs considerably from the rest. It is one of the few buildings to be seen that date from Period II. Two architectural sections are apparent: the lower one, or base,

The North Platform with its distinctive portico of double columns and vertical walls.

21

is arrow-shaped; the second has stone slabs with reliefs representing the places conquered by the governors of Monte Albán. Some of these stones are in fact "dancers" dating from Period I, from Structure L ("The Dancers"), which were reused. An 80 cm wide tunnel runs through the upper section, but its purpose has not been discovered. By contrast, it has been ascertained that the point of the building indicates the direction in which five of the 25 brightest stars are due to sink to the horizon in a few hours. This has made experts sure that it was an observatory.

Monte Albán was the most developed Zapotec city; no other approached it in monumentality. There is no doubt that this sacred site attained the highest levels of purity in art. However, the Valley of Oaxaca is not confined to Monte Albán exclusively; other sites also show evidence of remarkable development, though more modestly. In any case, these sites that took on importance shortly after the decline of Monte Albán help to complete the historical scene. Their importance is then evident until the post-Classic era, when the Mixtec civilization begins to appear. We shall take a brief look at some of the important buildings in these smaller cities

Structure J (Valley of Oaxaca II) has an arrow shaped base.

(Mitla, Dainzú and Zaachila) that together give a more complete picture of what the Valley of Oaxaca was.

Mitla

The Columns Group. At Mitla there are two really striking constructions to see: the Columns Group and the Church Group. The first is a masterly work that combines Zapotec and Mixtec styles. It is composed of two quadrangles joined at one corner and lined on three sides by spacious chambers. The buildings it contains are located separately on independent platforms. The north building is the most attractive to look at; inside there is a large room measuring 7×38 meters, with a row of six monolithic columns running down the center. The courtyards are particularly brilliant, being decorated with the

Both pictures show the skillful carving of the walls of Mitla.

typical Mitla fret pattern. In this system, a wall of stones held together with mud was erected, then hundreds of small, cut stones were applied to it to form the mosaic. Such decoration, involving great effort, allows a wide variety of motifs. More than 100,000 cut stones are calculated to have been used in Mitla.

The Church Group. Its layout is very similar to that of the preceding building, but it is smaller. One of its courtyards disappeared when the Church was built over it. So, the only feature to be seen is the north court, surrounded by rooms that very probably used to be decorated with murals. Today only one band, painted in the Mixtec style, survives. The architectural style of both complexes is notably different from what we have seen earlier. This change is of course due to the Mixtecs.

Zaachila

This was the last capital of the Zapotecs (later conquered by the Mixtecs). The names of a series of governors is known, and Zaachila also won importance with the fall of Monte Albán. There is one large pyramid on this site, right in the center of the present village, which has not been explored properly. In 1962, when a certain mound with several chambers was examined, two tombs were discovered. The first was decorated with two feline heads on the threshold; in the antechamber depictions of owls and two personages bearing the inscriptions of 5 Flower and 9 Flower were discovered. At the back appeared another figure whose head emerges from a serpent and whose body resembles a turtle shell. The tomb contained and offering rich, in Mixtec-style pottery. The second tomb yielded gold items such as rings (one of them still on the ring finger of a left hand), beads, repoussé work and jade fan stems. The Mixtecs were master goldsmiths and jewelers.

Dainzú

Although Dainzú was a large town, only three buildings have been excavated. The largest one is a pyramidal base with a series of stone bas-reliefs on the south side showing ball-game players, in violent attitudes, who probably also symbolize the four deities of the game: two men and two jaguars. There is some slight resemblance between these figures and the "dancers". They belong to Period V.

Another example of the Mixtec goldsmith's artistry.

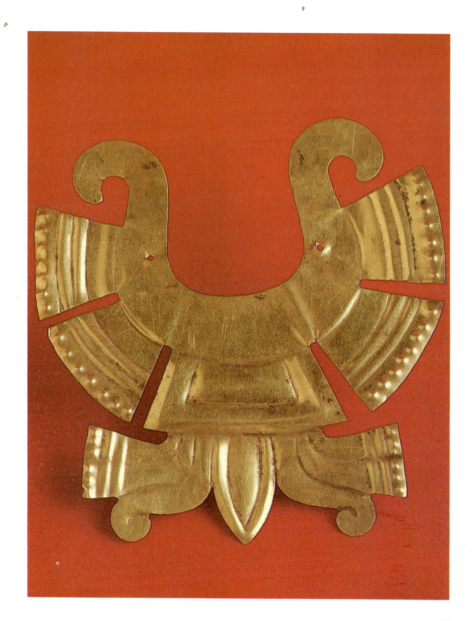

A little lower, after a building with spacious courtyards and numerous chambers, there is a ball court —partly reconstructed— that can be dated to around 1,000 A.D. Because of this late dating it can be said to have no relationship with the bas-reliefs we have just seen.

Lambityeco

When the Pan-American highway was being built a mound was noticed casually: it was Lambityeco. This led in 1961 to the start of archaeological investigations that terminated in 1968 with the discovery of a pyramid since known as Mound 195. Lambityeco is important for the study of Period IV (in Period V it no longer existed as a city). The pyramidal forms that are to be seen here show frequent use of the vertical wall (tablero) that must be interpreted as a tradition continued from Monte Albán. Another outstanding feature at Lambityeco is stucco sculpture, of which three types have been discovered: one, the enormous busts of Cocijo, the Zapotec rain god, with the characteristic urn shape; the one used for modeling human heads, a little larger than lifesize; and the one found in the magnificent friezes with

Like that of Monte Albán, the Ball Court of Dainzú has sloping platforms.

glyphs and human figures at the back of a courtyard where a tomb was discovered.

One of the most important civilizations of Mesoamerica took root in the Valley of Oaxaca. In this highly developed world Zapotecs and Mixtecs left, more than anything else, impressive monumental architecture. Investigation into the meaning and importance of their cultures is bound to continue.

Cocijo, Zapotec god of rain.